Scholastic
First Biographies™

Let's Read About...
Squanto

by Sonia W. Black
Illustrated by Bob Doucet

Cartwheel
·B·O·O·K·S·®

SCHOLASTIC INC.
New York   Toronto   London   Auckland   Sydney
Mexico City   New Delhi   Hong Kong   Buenos Aires

Let's Read About...
Squanto

For Johanna
— S.W.B.

For Stephanie
— B.D.

The editors would like to thank Joyce E. Chaplin,
Professor of History at Harvard University, for her expertise.

ISBN 0-439-45952-4

Text copyright © 2002 by Sonia W. Black.
Illustrations copyright © 2002 by Bob Doucet.

All rights reserved. Published by Scholastic Inc.

SCHOLASTIC, CARTWHEEL BOOKS, and associated logos are trademarks
and/or registered trademarks of Scholastic Inc.

Library of Congress Cataloging-in-Publication Data available

12 11 10 9 8 7 6 5 4 3 2   2 3 4 5 6 7/0

Printed in the U.S.A.
First printing, November 2002

A Native American boy named
Tisquantum (Tis-qwan-tum)
was born long ago around 1591.
His home was the village of
Patuxet (Paw-tu-ket).
Tisquantum was a bright, happy boy.

The Patuxet people belonged to
the Wampanoag (Wam-pa-no-ag) Nation.
They lived in the forest
in the fall and winter.

They hunted deer, beaver, wild turkey,
and other animals for food.
Young Tisquantum went hunting, too.

They moved the village closer to the ocean
in the spring and summer.
They planted corn, squash, beans,
and other vegetables.

The Native Americans fished for food, too.
Tisquantum went fishing with his
friends one day.
Someone shouted, "Look!"

There was a big ship in the water.
Strange men came ashore.
They were English traders.
They spotted Tisquantum and his friends.

The strangers spoke a different language.
But Tisquantum understood their
friendly actions.
"We'll call you Squanto," they said.
They invited Squanto to sail home
with them.

It was 1605.
Squanto was fourteen years old.
He wanted an adventure.
He sailed off to England.

Squanto lived with Sir
Ferdinando Gorges.
He was the owner of the ship.
Sir Gorges taught Squanto
how to speak English.

In 1614, Sir Gorges hired Squanto
as a guide to travel with his sea captains.
The men were returning to explore
the new land.
Squanto would talk to the Natives
for them.
Squanto had been gone for nine years.
"It will be good to go home," he said.

Squanto was a very smart guide.
He led Captain John Smith
through many new territories.
He helped him to draw up maps.
He traded with Natives.

Squanto's life suddenly changed one day.
He was taken prisoner by Captain
Thomas Hunt.
Captain Hunt took Squanto to Spain.
The captain sold him as a slave.

Kind monks bought Squanto
and set him free.
They helped him get
on another ship.

It was 1619 when Squanto returned to his village.
It was empty.
Squanto was all alone.
He went to live in another Wampanoag village nearby.

It was a spring day in 1621.
Squanto's friend Samoset
brought him news about his old village.
"English settlers have been living
there since the winter," Samoset said.
"They call themselves Pilgrims."

Samoset took Squanto to meet the Pilgrims.

The Pilgrims had sailed from
Plymouth, England.
They came on a ship called the *Mayflower*.
They called this new land, *New* England.
The old Patuxet village was now
called Plymouth.

The Pilgrims had suffered during the
terrible, cold winter.
They had very little food.
Squanto felt sorry for them.
"I will live with you and help you," he said.

Squanto brought the Wampanoag chief
to meet the Pilgrims' governor.
The chief was angry with settlers
for taking the Native Americans' land.
Some settlers had also treated them badly.
Squanto wanted to make peace.

Governor John Carver promised the Pilgrims
would be kind to the Wampanoags.
Chief Massassoit (Mass-a-soit)
promised to protect the Pilgrims from
harmful Natives.

Squanto taught the Pilgrims many things. He taught them better ways to plant crops. He showed them which wild berries were safe to eat.

He taught them how to set traps to fish, to dig for clams, and to catch eel and lobster.
He also helped them to hunt.

The Pilgrims had a good harvest that fall.
There was enough food to last all winter.
They decided to have a feast to
give thanks.
Chief Massassoit came with ninety men.

They brought five deer for roasting.
There was also duck, goose, and turkey.
There were fish, vegetables, and berries.
The happy celebration lasted for
three long days.
This was the first Thanksgiving.

Squanto's Pilgrim friends loved
him very much.
They would not have made it without him.
Squanto was a great Wampanoag.
He played a big part in building
Plymouth colony.